Unplugging Your Mind
Guided Meditations to Relax, Rest and Renew

Unplugging Your Mind
Guided Meditations to Relax, Rest and Renew

Leslie Lyn Hi'ialo Harrington
Yoga Therapist & Master Yoga Teacher Trainer
Certified Health Coach, Certified Personal Trainer & E-RYT-500

Dedication

This book is dedicated to all of you who desire a respite from their stress and the constant stream of thoughts so that they can find their way to relax, rest and renew.

"What you seek is seeking you."

—RUMI

Copyright © 2018 by Leslie Harrington, Phoenix, Arizona.

Back Cover Photography by Robert Behnke

Design by Leslie Harrington, Edited By Patty Garcia-Likens

No part of this publication may be reproduced, stored in a retrieval system or transmitted in any form or by any means, electronic, mechanical, photocopying, recording, scanning, or otherwise, except as permitted under Sections 107 or 108 of the 1976 United States Copyright Act, without the prior written permission of the Publisher. Requests to the Publisher for permission should be addressed to Iron Belle Fitness, LLC Attn: Permissions Department, 4111 E Capistrano Ave, Phoenix, Arizona 85044. Limit of Liability/Disclaimer of Warranty: The Publisher and the author make no representations or warranties with respect to the accuracy or completeness of the contents of this work and specifically disclaim all warranties, including without limitation warranties of fitness for a particular purpose. No warranty may be created or extended by sales or promotional materials. The advice and strategies contained herein may not be suitable for every situation. This work is sold with the understanding that the publisher is not engaged in rendering medical, legal, or other professional advice or services. If professional assistance is required, the services of a competent professional person should be sought.

Neither the Publisher nor the author shall be liable for damages arising there from. The fact that an individual, organization, or website is referred to in this work as a citation and/or potential source of further information does not mean that the author or the Publisher endorses the information the individual, organization, or website may provide or recommendations they/it may make. Further, readers should be aware that Internet websites listed in this work may have changed or disappeared between when this work was written and when it is read.

All rights reserved.

ISBN-10:   1985827867   ISBN-13: 978-1985827868

Table of Contents

Dedication	1
Table of Contents	3
Introduction	5
Why Guided Meditation?	9
How to Do Guided Meditation	11
Guided Meditations	15
1. Your Favorite Place to Be	16
2. Body Relaxation	19
3. Quietest Place on Earth	22
4. Garden of Flowers	24
5. Healing Light Meditation	26
6. Sunflower Meditation	28
7. Floating Balloons	30
8. Energy Balancing	33
9. Stilling Pond	37
10. Crystal Lake	40
11. New Paths	43
12. Footprints In The Sand	46
13. Peaceful Evening Sky	48
14. Butterfly (Great for Kids too!)	50

Introduction

One of the first things I hear my in meditation workshops and in my health coaching is "How do I stop my mind from thinking all the time?" or "I can't seem to turn my mind off at night." Often not finding peace of mind means a recipe for stress, worry, and anxiety. If you can relate, you are not alone. One great tool to help resolve these concerns is meditation.

Perhaps you think that meditation isn't exactly your style of things. Or, maybe when you think of meditation you picture a yogi sitting on top of a mountain in some foreign land wearing saffron-colored robes. That is far from the truth. Over the years, I have helped hundreds of people find a type of meditation that works for them, and believe it or not there are many styles of meditation to discover.

What is great is that there is not just one meditation technique that works for everyone in every situation. A different technique might work great for one person and not resonate with another. So, keep looking… just because you have tried one style of meditation and it didn't feel good at that time in your life or situation, you can still find a meditation that will resonate with you. It is kind of like saying you watched a movie once and didn't like it so all movies aren't good. However, there are different types of movies; like documentaries, romantic comedies, action/adventure, etc., that might be more your style.

Guided meditations happen to be one of the easiest ways to start a mindfulness or meditation practice. After using guided meditation at night, one of my health coaching clients no longer needed her sleep and anxiety medications that she had been using for years. The only trouble now is if she does a guided meditation during the middle of her work day it has conditioned her to fall asleep. So we then had to get her another meditation style to use during the day. Great problem to have, am I right?

I was first exposed to guided meditations in a leadership training when I was 12 years old. The way that the instructor had set up the whole lesson plan seemed like just a fun activity to do. All the students got to draw and color their favorite place to be in the world, a place where we felt the most relaxed and at peace. The drawing didn't have to be perfect, it was just designed to make us think about some of the details so that we could really picture it. The instructor then she turned off the lights and had us sit upright in our classroom chairs with our feet on the ground and our hands folded comfortably on our laps and she walked us through a guided meditation. I got to experience the beautiful benefits of meditation for the first time and I was hooked. You'll get to experience the same thing with the first mediation, called Your Favorite Place To Be (page 16). I've since used this technique myself and with friends who couldn't sleep or just needed to relax.

So, when I became a yoga instructor I naturally started using this meditation technique at the end of all of my yoga classes. People seem to love it, especially when they had no experience with the typical yoga final resting pose (shavasana). It is said, that for the Western culture shavasana can be the most challenging yoga pose of all. Think of it, what was the last time you had silent around you? When did you select to have some quite time with no TV or radio around or external distraction?

People are not used to being quiet with just their thoughts anymore. There are constant options for input and distractions with all the access to technology and information around like movies and music on demand and Google™ or YouTube™ on every smart phone.

In this book, I will be going over various guided meditations that I have created and clients have effectively used over the years. I hope you'll be able to experience the relaxation, rest and renewal as they have.

Now let's get started…

Why Guided Meditation?

Meditation had been used for thousands of years. And in recent years, meditation has been scientifically proven to be cathartic and healing for the body and mind. In the frantic and overstimulated world, it seems even harder to do and yet has become even more necessary.

Guided meditation allows you to picture yourself in a situation and get immersed in a reservoir of positivity and letting go of the constant stream of thoughts at that moment — a mental and physical break for even a few minutes. Being able to take this time for yourself leads to physical and emotional health benefits:

Psychological Benefits
- Improve cognitive functions
- Enhance creativity
- Improve problem-solving skills
- Decrease depression and anxiety
- Promote a positive outlook

Physical Benefits
- Decrease levels of stress hormones
- Boosting immune system
- Reduce muscular tension
- Reduced risk of heart disease
- Improve sleep quality

Emotional Benefits
- Improved sense of positivity
- Increased confidence
- Greater ability to give and receive love
- Elimination of panic attacks
- A greater sense of warmth and openness towards others

Spiritual Benefits
- Better connection with others
- Create a greater sense of purpose and meaning
- Improve intuition
- An openness to love and to higher guidance
- Let go of stress and negativity

How to Do Guided Meditation

There is no wrong way to do guided meditation unless you just are not comfortable. So, first of all, you need to get comfy. You don't need to be sitting in lotus pose crossed legged on the floor. (However, if this is comfortable, you can add support with a blanket under each knee or a yoga block behind the hips up against a wall if you like.) Just start by sitting back in your chair or lying back comfortably on a sofa or bed with your eyes closed. If you are seated, try having your feet resting on the ground and sitting with a stacked spine. Your hands can rest on your lap or by your side with the palms facing up to be open and receptive to what is to come. Or hands palms down to feel more grounded. It all depends on what you need for the day. Some days you will want perhaps more grounding and other days more openness.

Many of the great thinkers in history would take a short 20 minutes out of their day to "recharge their batteries" but doing an easy meditation just sitting upright in a comfortable chair.

Your Breath: The best way to breath for any style of meditation is in and out through the nose. If you can breathe in and out of your nose; this helps to humidify and detoxify the air as well as focus your awareness in the present moment. However, if this is not comfortable, breathing in any manner is great. When you breathe in, you should be expanding into the abdomen. And as you breathe out the abdomen should be relaxing inward. This is called the diaphragmatic breath, as you are using the strength of the diaphragm. This might feel odd at first as it is opposite of what many adults do naturally. If you have ever watched a baby or puppy sleep, their bellies rise and fall with the breath. Breathing with just the chest moving is a shallow breath. This is also called the stress breath as it activates the sympathetic nervous system; which is the system to turn on the fight or flight response within the body. But breathing into the belly is the way to get you the deepest relaxing breath possible and help to turn on your "rest and renew nervous system," which is also known as the parasympathetic nervous system. If this is challenging try placing your hands on the abdomen and bringing your awareness here. Or lie on your abdomen to feel the rise and fall of your breath.

Guided Meditations

~Free Companion Audio Guided Meditations~

To download and listen to all of the guided meditations included with this book please visit the following link:

https://ironbellefitness.com/14meditationdownloads

1. Your Favorite Place to Be

Optional: The first time you do this meditation start by taking a few minutes to sketch, with some colored pencils, the scene of your favorite place to be. It doesn't have to be perfect or take too long at all. It helps to add some details in your mind for the meditation itself.

Getting comfortable, sitting or lying back comfortably with your eyes closed. Taking a deep breath, perhaps the deepest breath of the day so far. Breathing in through the nose and breathing out through the nose. Feeling your belly rise and fall with each breath. Breathing fully into the torso and now breathing fully into the whole body. Out to the fingers and then toes and all the spaces between.

Now starting to imagine your favorite place to be. Somewhere quiet, somewhere where peaceful. Perhaps your favorite vacation spot. Perhaps, lying on a secluded beach. Or curled up under a warm blanket on a rainy day. Or under some trees atop a mountain. Or even perhaps floating among the softest clouds in the sky. Your favorite place can be real or imaginary. Perhaps a place you have only seen in a picture or even in a dream.

Now start to imagine all the colors that surround you here. What are you resting on? Can you feel the sand beneath you? Or the soft cool grass or the most comfortable feathered bed? And imagine the perfect temperature here. Perhaps a gentle breeze to cool you, or the warmth of the sun on your skin. And now starting to listen to the sounds here in your favorite place. Do you hear a bird call in the distance? Or perhaps some water moving close by? The soft ocean waves or a gentle stream? Or the perfect sound of silence?

Continuing to breathe in and out. Feeling more and more relaxed every inhalation and exhalation. Breathing in feeling more content and breathing out feeling more at peace. Staying here for as long as you like. And when you are ready you can start to bring your awareness back to your body. Moving a finger or toe at first. And knowing you can take this feeling with you the rest of the day. Taking a deep stretch with your arms reaching out overhead. Feeling rested and ready for the day.

2. Body Relaxation

You start by lying on your back or sitting comfortably, with your spine stacked up in an upright position. Take a few moments to relax and let go of the stress and knots of tension. You start to feel the weight of your body pulled to the ground, and yet you feel light.

Inhaling and you feel that your body becomes lighter. Exhaling and you feel gravity taking over. With each moment, each breath, you let go and start to relax. Letting each breath be a wave of relaxation over you.
Starting to relax each muscle as you go. You start to surrender your muscles from the crown of your head

and down through the entire head and then encircling the eyes and moving down around the jaws. Breath by breath you continue to move down into the neck and the shoulders. Continuing down the body, releasing and relaxing as you go. Next, the releasing and relaxing muscles in your shoulders and arms and down and out to the hands and all the fingers. Letting go of any of the remaining stress or tension. Softening with each and every breath a bit more, relaxing a little more.

Continuing by inhaling and exhaling and relaxing your chest, back, abdomen, and lower back. Now relaxing into the hips, releasing and relaxing here. Let the tension melt in to the earth. Breathing slowly and feeling your legs relaxing. Surrender the muscles in your upper legs and thighs.

Moving down behind the knees and encircling the kneecaps and moving the breath into the lower legs. Let the stress fall away from your calves and finally, from your ankles, feet, and out of your toes.

Your body is completely relaxed, completely at peace. Your mind is completely relaxed, completely at peace. Your heart is completely relaxed, completely at peace. You are free to stay here as long as you like to.

You enjoy every second you stay here. There is no place like right now at this very moment, and you savor it.

Slowly, when you are ready, you can start to bring your mind back to your body. Becoming aware of yourself. Move your fingers and toes or gently nod your head from side to side.

Stretching your hands over your head like a deep morning stretch from your fingers to your toes. Take your time, and follow the pace that you are comfortable with, and slowly come back to the present moment where you are.

3. Quietest Place on Earth

Start by sitting or lying back comfortably with your eyes closed.

Taking a deep breath. In through the nose. Out through the nose. Feeling your abdomen rise and fall with each inhalation and exhalation.

Starting to notice any sounds around you. A sound close by. The sound of the air conditioning fan or the buzz of electronics near you. And staying with that sound for a few breaths. Focusing your attention there and listening to the sound beneath the sounds. Now bring your attention to a sound further away. Perhaps a song of a bird in the distance. Or the sound of a plane flying overhead. Now listening to the sound beneath the sounds. The sound of silence. The quiet and the calm that is there with everything.

Now starting to imagine yourself transported to one of the quietest places on earth, to the middle of a crater in a dormant volcano mountain park on a beautiful island in Hawaii. This mountain stands around 2,000 meters high, with the crater about 800 meters deep. The walls of the crater gently slope up to create this protection from the world beyond. So quiet, so peaceful; there isn't even the sound of wind or animals. The sounds of the world fade away.

Breathing in and out. Feeling more and more quiet and centered with each breath. Feeling perfectly serene and peaceful. You can stay here for as long as you like. And when you are ready you can start to bring out awareness back to your body. Moving a finger or toe. And knowing you can take this quiet and calm with you the rest of the day as it always resides within you.

4. Garden of Flowers

Slowly take a deep breath in and releasing your breath and now closing your eyes. Relaxing your eyes. Relaxing your face. And relaxing your whole body. Letting the breath center you in the moment.

Now starting to imagine an exquisite garden with endless flowers everywhere in every direction you can see. Imagining yourself walking further into the garden step-by-step. Feeling the soft green grass under your feet. Slowly stopping along the way to look at each and every one of the flowers in this beautiful garden. The colors are so vibrant and each one seems to be telling you to have a great day.

Seeing a white orchid with lines of purple and it is so soft and appealing. It seems it is there to calm you and protect you. You breathe in the fragrance and it is like a special perfume of sweetness. Taking a moment or two to let the smell surround you.

Next gazing over, you see a soft pale yellow and white flower and it is reminiscent of the color of a new sunrise. It seems it is there to renew you and remind you of how amazing life can be. You breathe in the fragrance and it is like a special perfume of spring, of new beginnings. You are so refreshed and renewed. Taking a moment or two to let the smell surround you.

Enjoying your time here in the garden of flowers. You let your eye fall upon another flower. What color is it? And what lovely fragrance does it have? And what great feeling does it bring to your mind? How would you like to feel today?

Staying in this garden of flowers for as long as you like. And when you are ready, starting to return your awareness back to the present moment. Opening your eyes with the knowledge that you can go to your garden in your mind anytime you want the relax and renew.

5. Healing Light Meditation

Taking a deep breath in releasing your breath and closing your eyes.

Start by lying back and getting comfortable, so comfortable that you can be here for a few moments. Breathing in and breathing out, relaxing a little more with each breath.

Taking a breath deep into the lungs fully. And as you exhale letting go of that air fully. On your next inhalation imagining the breath filling your entire body, out to your fingers and toes. And as you exhale, imagining the body relaxing a little more.

Now starting to envision a beautiful healing white light at the center of your body. With every breath, this healing white light starts to radiate and grow bigger and bigger. Imagining that white light filling the entire body and every space in between.

This white light is so bright it radiates and heals any areas of the body that needs any special attention. Focusing your breath in this area a little longer if you need. Taking a deep breath in and a deep breath out that healing white light starts to grow and expand in all directions taking a deep breath in a deep breath out that healing white light starts to expand beyond the body, growing in all directions. Now letting that white light completely envelope and surround the entire body and expand beyond.

Breathing in and out. Feeling more and more renewed with each breath. Feeling regenerated and restored. You can stay here for as long as you like. And when you are ready you can start to bring out awareness back to your body. Moving a finger or toe. Taking a deep stretch with your arms reaching out overhead, knowing you can take this renewed feeling with you the rest of the day.

6. Sunflower Meditation

Closing your eyes, taking a deep breath in and releasing your breath. Relaxing your eyes. Relaxing your face. And relaxing your whole body. Letting the breath center you in this very moment. Breathing in and breathing out.

Now starting to imagine hearing the ring of peace sounds of wind chimes far in the distance. Picturing yourself are in a sunny field and the afternoon sunlight dancing across the tall grasses. Gazing out across the field you see there are beautiful shoulder height sunflowers everywhere. Somehow you get the feeling you like you have been here before. Perhaps it feels so familiar that you must have come here often. You see your favorite sunflower and stop admire it. It is like it was meant for just you. You go to it and study the inner part of the flower, where you see a circular pattern, a pattern that makes you think about the circle of life. How everything is connected.

Breathing in and breathing out, you feel connected. Connected to everyone and everything in a new way. Studying this sunflower you see the universe in a new way. You know you matter and that you can radiate that same feeling to others. You are breathing in and out, feeling so relaxed and connected that you almost don't notice where your one breath begins or ends.

Breathing in and out. Feeling more and more relaxed and connected with each breath. You can stay here for as long as you like. And when you are ready, you can start to bring out awareness back to your body. Moving a finger or toe. Taking a deep stretch with your arms reaching out overhead, knowing you can take this relaxed and connected feeling with you the rest of the day and share it with others.

7. Floating Balloons

Begin with a comfortable position—lying on the ground or sitting back in a comfortable chair. A place where you can be relax for a few moments. Allowing yourself to take these few moments just for yourself.

Connecting to your breath, feeling your inhale, your belly expands and with your exhale your belly relaxes. Imagining your body as a balloon inflating and deflating with each breath. Observing as you breathe in through the nose and breathe out through the nose. Now let's slow down the balloon filling process, and match the deflating of the balloon to the same pace.

Now, every time you inhale, starting to imagine a balloon filling overhead with helium. As you exhale, the balloon gets tied with a string. Every inhale creates another balloon, and breath by breath, you will accumulate a bouquet of balloons overhead. Now starting to imagine the colors of these balloons…

Are they red? Or orange? Or yellow? Are they green or blue? Or are they indigo? Or even beautiful bright white?

Breath by breath, you become surrounded by a huge colorful bouquet of balloons, holding the strings to each in your hand. Soon, you start to feel your body lifting off from the ground and drifting serenely up in the sky.

What does the sky look like? Is it pale blue with soft sunlight sifting through the clouds? Or is it midnight ink-blue sky studded with stars?

Whatever the sky looks like, you feel light and peaceful, and you enter the infinite expanse above you. Reaching the perfect height in the sky and staying there for a while floating, observing your quiet and calm surroundings.

When you have taken your fill, you let loose one balloon at a time, breath by breath. Slowly, gently, starting to descend back to earth. You touch back to the ground light as a feather. You feel your body resting on the earth, and gravity slowly comes back to you. Feeling grounded and secure. Returning to the room you are in perhaps wiggling a finger or a toe, or nodding your head from side to side, and you are fully back. Ready for the day at hand.

What Colors Were Your Balloons?

Different colors represent different areas of your life where you may need/want some focus or balancing:

Red: Grounding/Stability and Security

Orange: Creativity and Passion for Life

Yellow: Will and Self Confidence

Green: Self Love and Relationships

Blue: Speaking Your Own Truth

Indigo: Wisdom and Intuition

White: Connection with Others and Source

8. Energy Balancing

About Energy Centers or Chakras: In many traditions, there are thoughts about energy centers which are called Chakras (Sanskrit for wheel or disc.) While not commonly known in traditional Western thought, the seven commonly used Chakras are located roughly over areas in the body called nerve bundles along the spine. For the purpose of this meditation, you can think of these as areas where a lot of information is taken in and sent out for the whole body, which can affect different systems of the body. Helping to heal these areas and unblock energy flow is a good thing.

Start by sitting on a comfortable chair or lying back on the ground with hands resting by your side. Connecting to your breath and focus on inhaling and exhaling. With every breath, you feel your anxieties and tensions dissolving away bit by bit.

Lengthening your breath, and extend the moments where you can find clarity and balance.

Starting to focus on the first chakra, the root chakra (Muladhara), which is located at the base of the spine. As you breathe, you imagine a red disc in this area rotating clockwise. Inhaling half a turn and exhaling half of the turn, every breath counts as one full revolution.

Just relax and feel the natural flow of your breathing and matching the rotation speed with it. With each turn of the red disc, say to yourself, "I am safe and secure."

Now moving to the next chakra, the sacral charka (Svadhishthana), which is located about two inches below the belly button. Imagining an orange disc rotating clockwise, half a turn as you inhale, and half a turn as you exhale. With every breath, you complete one rotation of the orange disc. Visualize the disc rotating smoothly without any resistance. Saying to yourself, "I experience joy and creativity." Inhaling half a turn and exhaling half of the turn, every breath counts as one full revolution. And when you are ready, you can move on to your next chakra.

The third chakra, the solar plexus chakra (Manipura) lies in the upper abdominal area, just below ribs. This time, imagine a disc the color of the sun, a warming yellow. Saying to yourself, "I am confident and radiant." Noticing how the disc rotates with every breath you take. Does it turn easy? Does it turn like a steady metronome?

When you complete your rotations, you move upwards to the fourth chakra, the heart chakra (Anahata) which lies at the center of your chest.

You move the bright emerald green disc through the smooth and easy rotations, inhaling half a turn and completing the rotation by exhaling. Saying to yourself, "I am love." Breathing in and breathing out.

You now move to the fifth chakra, the throat chakra (Vishudda), located in the center of the neck. And envisioning the disc to be a bright blue. Imagining the disc turns easily and does not resist against the turns at all. It all happens in a natural flow, while you feel a sense of calm washing over you. You say to yourself, "I speak my truth." Breathing in and breathing out.

Next, moving on to the sixth chakra, your third eye (Anja), located at the center of the forehead illuminated with the color indigo, like a deep evening sky. Saying to yourself, "I see the bigger picture." You stay here for seven rotations of the indigo disc. Breathing in and breathing out.

Finally, it is time that you move up to the seventh chakra, the chakra crown (Sahasrara), which is located right above the crown of your head. Envision a clear, white-colored bright disc, shaped like a flower with a thousand petals. You turn the beautiful disc clockwise with your breath. And saying to yourself, "I am" or "I am grateful for all the good things and people in my life." And as the disc turns, you start noticing that all the seven discs are rotating in synchronization. Feeling filled with a sensation of balance and feeling the colorful blend of harmony throughout your body.

Breathing in and out. Feeling balanced, harmonized and grounded. You can stay here for as long as you like. And when you are ready you can start to bring out awareness back to your body. Perhaps at first moving a finger or toe or even nodding your head from side to side. Taking a deep stretch with your arms reaching out overhead. And knowing you can take this balanced energy with you the rest of the day.

9. Stilling Pond

Begin by lying down in a comfortable position or sitting up in an easy position. Perhaps you have had a busy day or are preparing to head into your day. But for now, start by letting go of will happen or what has happened. Letting go of the minutes behind you or the hours to come but just allowing yourself to be free in this moment. Taking a deep breath in and a deep breath out. Often the busyness of the day keeps your body and mind moving so fast.

Just starting to allow yourself to start to slow down and enjoying an easy breath here. Imagine your body and mind, flowing just like a river. A fast-paced, flowing river picks up sediments along the way and becomes clouded. Unable to see through that water. To see what lies ahead. Just like yourself throughout the day, the mind, the body becomes cloudy.

Breathing in and out and slowing down the pace of your mind and body like slowing down the pace of the river. As the river slows, it turns into a stream. Noticing that the stream is calmer and quieter, and the sediment that you have picked up from thoughts and movements of the day is starting to settle down. Breathing in deeply and out deeply. Slowly, with each breath, the stream moves further along to finally flowing into a gentle pond.

In this pond, the water comes to a standstill. Any thoughts you have carried with you starts to settle. Like settling at the bottom of the pond, and the water, like your mind, becomes calm and clear. Just like the busy mind and the active body, you can slow down, too. Allowing your troubles to fall away. Allowing yourself to return to your true nature of calm and your true nature of clarity. Breathing in deeply and breathing out slowly.

Feeling more and more relaxed with each breath. Feeling calm. Enjoying the stillness within. You can stay here for as long as you like. And when you are ready you can start to bring out awareness back to your body, back to this day. Starting to find some movement into your body. Perhaps, beginning to move a finger or wiggling a toe or perhaps nodding your head side to side. Taking a deep stretch with your arms reaching out overhead to start anew, renewed and refreshed. And knowing you can take this calm, and this clarity you have found with you into the rest of the day. Have a beautiful day.

10. Crystal Lake

Relaxing and closing your eyes and focusing on your breathing. Feeling your belly rise and fall with every inhalation and exhalation. Every time you inhale, your belly rises and every time you exhale, your belly draws back in. Staying in this position for some time and breathing in and breathing out of your nose, or breathing in any way you are comfortable. Feeling grateful for taking this time for yourself.

Now, picturing yourself high up into the mountains. Imagine a coolness in the air surrounding you, appreciating the mountain air. As you gazing forward you see a crystal lake front of you. On the distant side of the lake are mountains topped with white beautiful snow. Starting to notice that the tall majestic lush green pine trees that surround the lake are swaying in the cool gentle breeze. You start to take notice of all the minute details of the trees—the glossy evergreen and brown clustered needles and even the ridges and points of the pinecones that sit atop the boughs. Maybe seeing the pinecones takes you to a memory of playing with them when you were younger and appreciating these moments. Taking a deep breath in and deep breath out.

Moving your gaze over this vast splendid view, the water of the lake catches your glance. First, noticing the photographic-like reflection of the snowcapped mountains, but as you focus, that image dissolves away, and you can now see to the bottom of the lake. The water is so clear, like a crystal, that you can perfectly see an old tree stump that had grown there before there was a lake. And you can see the smoothness of each rock in the depth of the water as you continue to look around.

When was the last time you took the time to slow down and notice the details in the moment? Allowing yourself to fully appreciate the opportunity to be fully present? Knowing that enjoying and noticing the details does not just have to be when you visit the lake.

Breathing fully in and fully out. Feeling more and more relaxed with each breath. Feeling refreshed and renewed. Enjoying the sense of gratitude, you feel for your surroundings and the breathtaking details of nature. You can stay here for as long as you like.

Only when you are ready, you can start to bring out awareness back to your breath and your body. While continuing to keep your eyes closes, starting to bring your attention back to the room you are in. Perhaps to find some moment in the body. Maybe moving a finger or moving a toe to help bring you back to your present surroundings. But knowing you can take this feeling of gratitude for allowing yourself to take this time for yourself. Perhaps taking a deep stretch with your arms reaching out overhead. It's going to be a good rest of the day.

11. New Paths

Start by sitting or lying back comfortably with your eyes closed. Taking a deep breathe in through the nose and out through the nose. Feeling the belly rise and fall with each breath. Making yourself a little more comfortable with each breathe. If you have outside thoughts flow in, using your focus on your breath to let those thoughts float on by. Those thoughts will be there later for you.

Breath by breath, imagining your thoughts floating away like clouds drifting by, and as the clouds dissipate, you start to envision a forest path appearing before you.

Walking down the path one step at a time, finding yourself moving among tall trees. The leaves of the trees dancing lightly to let dapples of sunlight through the canopy. The air is warm around you but the gentle breeze that is moving the leaves of the trees is soft and cool. Off in the distance, you can hear a songbird singing its melodic tune. With each step you take you notice the cushion of green moss and slight rustling of newly fallen leaves.

As you continue walking, you soon notice you are walking in one direction, a path of sorts, which you continue down until it leads you to an opening among the trees, a clearing. There, you find a crossing of many paths—as many as your hopes, your goals and your dreams.

The opportunities waiting for you along this road excite you, and you can't wait to move along. But to move forward, you need to lighten your load, to let go of the baggage you carried with you; your something from your past.

This is the opportunity to let go of those things that you perhaps you carried unnecessarily. Perhaps things that you thought were keeping you safe or you needed just because. Or perhaps you didn't realize you carried along the way. They may have served a purpose in the past, but now it is time to move on to explore new opportunities waiting for you. Breath in, taking an inhale deep into the belly and an exhaling, letting your belly fall. With that breath you decide what you can leave behind and another breath helps you decide which path to move forward on. The one to the left or right or straight ahead. It doesn't matter which path you choose because it is more about the journey. And enjoying the moments along that path.

Feeling a sense of lightness and relief for letting go and sense of opportunity for your next journey. Just knowing you are on your right path. Experiencing the journey, you choose for your own life.

You can stay here for as long as you like. And when you are ready, you can start to bring out awareness back to your body. Perhaps moving a finger or a toe to bring you back to your current surroundings and keeping your eyes closed for a moment longer. Beginning to take a deep stretch with your arms reaching out overhead. Starting to open your eyes, with the knowledge you can take this sense of letting go and opportunity of enjoying the journey with you the rest of the day. Have a beautiful rest of the day.

12. Footprints In The Sand

Lying back in a comfortable position. Closing your eyes and focusing on your breath. Inhaling through your nose and exhaling through your nose. Breathing in, your belly rises and expands in all directions, front, back and to the sides. Breathing out, your belly retracts easily. Breath by breath, slowing your breath down. Once you get into a rhythm, start to imagine your breath like soft waves coming gently to a shore.

Breath by breath, wave by wave, your breath like the gentle ocean waves, washes in and out. On the inhale, imagine the waves lapping up on to the shore of a sandy beach. On the exhale, imagine the waves going back into the sea.

Picturing your mind as the surface of the beach. The footprints on the surface of the beach are like your thoughts tracking across your mind. A wave comes in and washes away the footprint, leaving behind the smooth sand. Just like your every breath, the thoughts wash away, leaving behind calmness and tranquility.

With each breath you take, your mind becomes clearer. Fewer footprints on the beach of your mind.

Feeling a sense of calm and peace in your mind. You can lie here for as long as you like.

When you are ready you can start to bring out awareness back to your body. Perhaps starting to return to the room, you can keep your eyes closed for a moment longer and begin by finding some movement in the body; by moving a finger or a toe or even nodding your head from side to side. Taking a deep stretch with your arms reaching out overhead you can start to open your eyes as you are rest. And just knowing you can take this feeling of calmness and tranquility with you the rest of the day. Have a most beautiful rest of the day.

13. Peaceful Evening Sky

Sitting in a comfortable position starting to relax, to find some ease for the day. Starting to connect with your body. Tuning into how you are feeling. Just noticing what is going on inside of you; observing your thoughts. What has the constant stream of thought brought you today?

When you are ready, close your eyes and focus on your breathing. The feeling every time you inhale is that your belly rising. Every time you exhale, your belly relaxes. Stay in this position for some time and breathe in and out through your nose, or any way you are comfortable with.

Now imagine the deep color of an evening sky above you. Perhaps shades of blue, indigo or violet, and gazing over toward the sun setting below the horizon with the fading of the last colors of pink, orange and yellow. Slowly the remains of the sunset dissipate. And all that remains is the ever-deepening blue. Starting to notice the glint of one star above and breath by breath the sky grows deeper into the night and more stars start to appear. A few so bright, these must be distant planets. What a beautiful sense of calm expands through your body. Like the expanse of the sky. You don't even feel there is a separation between where you begin and where the sky ends.

Feeling a sense of calm and peace in your mind. You can stay here for as long as you like.

When you are ready, bringing your awareness back to your body. Then finding some movement into the body, maybe wiggling a finger or a toe at first. Taking a deep stretch with your arms reaching out overhead. Knowing you can take this feeling with you the rest of the day.

14. Butterfly (Great for Kids too!)

Lying back as if you are pretending that you are sleeping. Imaging what you look like when you are sleeping? Are you curled up? Do you lie down with your hand over your eyes? Can you fool your sibling or your parents that you are sleeping? Closing your eyes and holding very still. Does your breath slow as you fall asleep? Maybe trying a slower breath. Inhaling slowly and exhaling slowly.

Making yourself comfortable. Now imagining an easy sunny day and spending the day going on a picnic. First, walking among rolling pastures. The young green blades of grass are soft but tall. Easily, you find a place on the hill with a view of outstretched hills. Spotting off in the distance, a few trees that must be near a stream.

Sitting on a cushy blanket, the high grass creates almost low walls around the blanket carving out a private space just for you. This space lets you feel safe and protected. Like a private escape belonging only to you. Sitting down on the blanket, it calls for you to lie back and rest. Taking a breath in and slowly exhaling, you feel like you could sink back into the blanket even more. Looking up to see just the light powdery blue sky above with a few clouds dusted across your view. Noticing out of the corner of your eye, over at the top is the grass; an orange butterfly with black dotted wings making its way toward you. Holding still so the butterfly won't fly away just yet. Oddly enough you think to yourself the butterfly is moving gently toward you. Then remembering that you had picked a pretty purple flower during your walk in the pastures and that you still have it in your hand. Knowing that if you don't move you might have a chance to have the pretty insect land close by. Breathing slow and smoothly, the butterfly lands gently on the petals of your handheld flower. What a treat to be so close to seeing all the details of the butterfly. Though many look similar, no two butterflies have the exact same pattern. Seeing the beauty of the smallest of things; the edge of a blade of grass; the petal of the flower the butterfly sits atop. Even the way the light little legs of the butterfly dancing across the flower.

Feeling a sense of awe and tranquility flowing through your body, mind and heart. You breathe slowly, really just enjoying this space, just for yourself. Taking it all in. Knowing that you can stay here as long as you like. There is no other place you need to be then right here, right now. You can lie here for as long as you like.

When you are ready you can start to bring out awareness back to your body. Finding some movement, a finger or toe perhaps. Maybe reaching your arms overhead like taking a deep morning stretch. Feeling that you can take the tranquility with you the rest of the day.

~Namaste
The light in me honors and respects the light in you.

Meet Leslie Harrington
Speaker, Corporate Wellness Consultant & Fitness Coach

After many years in the corporate world, **Leslie Harrington** (CHC, CPT & C-IAYT) realized that her passion is helping people with their health and wellness. In 2007, she started Iron Belle Fitness, L.L.C. where she brings specialized wellness programming to her private and corporate clients. Leslie also leads fitness and yoga teacher trainings around the world and speaks at health and wellness conferences around the county. She loves being able to share the joys and benefits of health and wellness.

Education and Achievements

- Registered Yoga Teacher E-RYT-500, Yoga Therapist, and Ayurveda Lifestyle Coach
- International Yoga Teacher Trainer & Speaker
- Certified Holistic Health & Nutrition Coach (CHC) & Certified Personal Trainer (CTP)
- Bachelor's Degree in Communications

TO FIND OUT HOW YOU CAN WORK WITH
Leslie Lyn Hi'ialo Harrington
Visit www.IronBelleFitness.com

Made in the USA
San Bernardino, CA
03 August 2018

Made in the USA
San Bernardino, CA
03 August 2018